1990s]
Flashback

MATT ZEIGLER

ISBN-13: 978-1478283614
ISBN-10:1478283610

DEDICATION

This work is dedicated to my wife, Glenda.

Grant Hill

CONTENTS

Chapter 1 Air Jordan

Air Jordan; the name was much more than an ultra-successful marketing campaign. It represented athleticism, power, speed, excitement, an iron will and basketball skills that bordered on perfection. Show-stopping action and great performances defined Jordan's career and dominated the National Basketball Association in the 1990s. Be it a 7-footer in the post; a 6-7/6-8 double-team on the perimeter; the flu; nothing stopped vintage Air Jordan.

Year-in and year-out, night-in and night-out, Michael 'Air' Jordan was the star attraction of the greatest team in sports. It all began with a fury in 1984 when Jordan took off into NBA stardom with the Chicago Bulls. With an energetic, slam-dunking style the 6'-6" shooting guard exploded onto the scene. Jordan could drop jumpers, drive to the basket and finish with a spectacular move; or draw a file for free-throw attempts. And when needed Jordan would jump over anybody in his way and finish with a power slam. He was also a playmaker who dished-out assists and played lockdown defense. The young Jordan was all just a sampling to what would become the most dominant and respected athletic career on the planet, and later named by ESPN as the Greatest Athlete of The 20th Century.

Early in his career Jordan became legendary for a game-winning shot: a jumper in 1982 as a freshman for North Carolina to win the NCAA Tournament. Even after a becoming an All-American and Player of the Year as a junior, Jordan exceeded all expectations as a pro, beginning with averaging 28.2 points per game his rookie year. And that game-winning shot Jordan produced in the '82 NCAA Finals became his signature in the pros as well, along with winning multiple championships.

However, it wouldn't be a smooth climb to the top of the NBA ranks for MJ. Despite the enormous success of Jordan his rookie year, the Bulls

9

remained mired in losing, posting a 38-44 record in '84-85. Jordan's second NBA season promised to be even better, until a foot injury put him out of action for all but 18 games of the regular season. Jordan made it back before the year was out and his offensive heroics climbed to even a higher level during the '86 playoffs of that ill-fated season. He poured in an NBA playoff record 63 points in a losing cause against the Boston Celtics in an epic night 'in the zone.' It was a truly remarkable performance in that Boston defended Jordan with 7-foot Robert Parish, 6'-10" Kevin McHale and 6-9 Larry Bird but Jordan destroyed them all.

Jordan's was on fire during the '86-87 season, averaging a league-high 37.1 points per game to go along with All-Star selection, the Slam Dunk Championship and a slew of other awards, which was a career-long standard. It was the first of seven consecutive years he'd lead the NBA in scoring; 10 years overall. Air Jordan continued to fly high the following season, to the outer limits of superstardom. He had absolutely the best and most entertaining "game" in the world, offense or defense.

The overall results from '87-88 show total dominance on an individual level: regular season MVP, scoring leader (35 ppg), Defensive Player of the Year, Slam Dunk Champion, All-Star Game MVP, plus the All-NBA Team. Jordan then had his typical 'A Game' season from tip-to-tip, whistle-to-whistle during the '88-89 campaign, averaging 32.5 points, 8 assists and rebounds, with 3 steals. All of which was accomplished with show-stopping style and total dedication to his game.

But even with Jordan on board the Bulls went through three consecutive losing seasons and first round playoff exits before going 50-32 in '87-88 and losing in the Eastern Conference semifinals. The Bulls initially lacked a solid lineup of teammates for Jordan and the coaching situation was all but stable; Jordan played for three different coaches before the elevation of Phil Jackson from assistant to head coach in 1989. The Bulls also brought in a higher caliber of talent to go alongside Jordan as he evolved into the NBA's best player during the late '80s.

The biggest addition of talent came in the 1987 Draft when Chicago got 6'-7" small forward Scottie Pippen and 6'-10" power forward Horace Grant. Another key addition to the Bulls came at the expense of Charles Oakley, who, after entering the league in 1985, had developed into a quality power forward. In return for Oakley, via a trade with the New York Knicks in 1988, Chicago got 7'1" center Bill Cartwright, a steady, if not spectacular, big man in the post. These additions helped Chicago to a 47-35 record in '88-89 but the Bulls were eliminated in the Conference Finals; and again the following season after going 55-27 with Jordan averaging 33.6 points a contest.

The Bulls were defeated in the Conference Finals both years by the eventual the NBA Champion Detroit Pistons, going down primarily because of the Pistons' physical style of play. Of course, aggressive defense and rebounding alone does not win titles; the Pistons had top-notch offensive performers the likes of Isaiah Thomas, Adrian Dantley, Vinnie "The Microwave" Johnson and Joe Dumars. Detroit also featured talented thugs in the form of Bill Laimbeer, Rick Mahorn and a young Dennis Rodman. And Isaiah, an all-time great at point guard, was no choirboy, as the word went in the NBA.

The high-flying, tongue-wagging youthful Jordan of the 1980s was guaranteed excitement, thrills and drama with more entertainment value than any athlete ever has attained. Every time he stepped on the court he delivered a first-rate performance. Be it a key block, breakaway highlight reel slam dunk, a steal or the last shot of the game for the win, Michael Jordan could do it all, game over. Yet, unlike most athletes, including some of the greatest ever, Jordan's level of play nor his overall accomplishments never slipped from the top echelon of his sport.

With all of his brilliance, his highlight reel library of moves and worldwide adulation, Jordan took his game to even a higher level in the 1990s with a run of two, back-to-back-to-back NBA Championships. Jordan was state-of-the-art, and he kept getting better and better. In addition, he did it with the same style, power and dominance that he displayed in his earlier years. But he also developed a killer instinct against all-comers in the playoffs. His dominating skills and knowledge of a savvy veteran enabled Jordan to conquer the sports world in the 1990s.

After years of futility it all came together for the Bulls in 1990-91 after they completed a 61-21 regular season and eventually met Detroit again in the Eastern Conference Finals. But by 1990 the golden age of Air Jordan was in full flight and the Bulls swept the Pistons 4-0. In the NBA Finals the Bulls faced the Los Angeles Lakers, led primarily by an injured Magic Johnson, and cruised to the title 4-1. Jordan began the decade with his usual brilliance: league MVP and scoring leader at 31.5 points per game, All-Star and First Team All-NBA on both offense and defense. The accolades included Jordan being named the Finals MVP, his first of six. When the Bulls took the court, especially in the Finals, Jordan always brought his absolute best game. In 179 career playoff games he averaged 33 points, with 6 rebounds and 6 assists.

However, greatness is not measured by just one title, not on Jordan's level, and the Bulls followed up their first championship with No. 2 in '91-92. And it was the usual platinum standard of outstanding production from Jordan. He was the NBA's scoring leader at 30.1 a game, Finals MVP, All-Star and all-everything in pro basketball, the unquestioned top gun in the NBA. Nobody else in the NBA came close to matching the greatness that was Air Jordan. Over the summer of 1992 Jordan was also part of the original "Dream Team," the US Olympic Basketball Team, which, for the first time ever, was comprised mostly of NBA players. The team's gold medal finish was MJ's second, to go along with the one he won in 1984.

Jordan was king of the Chicago Dynasty and the most respected and dominant athlete in any sport. Then he came back even stronger the next season in '92-93, leaving all challengers to the throne in his wake with 32.6 points per game and his usual file of awards, including another NBA title and Finals MVP award. With his legacy secure as a guarantee for the Naismith Hall of Fame (enshrined in 2009) Jordan switched games following the Bulls' third title in 1993, playing professional baseball with the White Sox organization, leaving behind the sport he dominated as its unquestioned best.

Jordan's father, James Jordan, was murdered during a robbery in the summer of 1993, casting a sad, dreary cloud over what had appeared to be a charmed life. But it wasn't the end of Jordan's NBA experience. Michael's baseball career would turn out to be short-lived and the aspiring outfielder didn't show immediate Major League talent, batting around .200 for the Birmingham Barons, a minor league club of the White Sox, with 30 steals in 1994. Regardless, no Minor Leaguer in the history of baseball generated as much media and fan attention as Jordan.

However, millions of fans worldwide wanted to see Jordan back in the NBA and he answered their wishes on March 19, 1995 when he returned, wearing No. 45 instead of his usual 23. Jordan's return, at age 31, created a frenzy but there were some skeptics who doubted if he could still perform at the highest level. Throughout the remainder of the regular season, Jordan averaged 26.9 in 17 games, including a game-winning jumper that April in Atlanta, and 55 points, his famous "double nickel," later on against New York at Madison Square Garden.

Jordan carried the Bulls through the playoffs with a 31.5 average. But the Orlando Magic, led by Shaquille O'Neal and Penny Hardaway, stopped the Bulls in the Eastern Conference Semifinals, which also saw the return of Jordan's No. 23. It was clear: Jordan wasn't his old self, not yet at least. The Bulls' failure to advance to the Finals gave the doubters plenty of cannon fodder, but Jordan came back with a vengeance the following year.

The Bulls' second dominant championship run of the decade featured mainstays Jordan and Pippen, plus a few new additions to the supporting cast, most notably former Detroit Piston Bad Boy Dennis Rodman. The 1995-96 Bulls were a well-tuned basketball machine that ran wild through the rest of the league with a 72-10 regular season, an NBA record; and ended the year with a 4-2 series win over Seattle in the Finals. Jordan dominated the NBA once again: league-leading 30.4 average, regular season, All-Star Game and Finals MVP, as wells as First Team All-NBA. Air Jordan was back in flight!

During his second championship run Jordan could still take defenders off the dribble and get the ball to the hoop with authority or with an agile move. And Jordan also developed the most deadly fadeaway jumper in the game during his second championship dynasty. Jordan used his incredible hang time to rise up and away from defenders to connect on a mid-to-long-range jumper. Jordan's fadeaway was a work of athletic art as he floated in midair away from the outstretched arms of the opposition.

There was no stopping Jordan and the Bulls as they went for championship No.5 in '96-97 with a 69-13 record before defeating Utah 4-2 in the Finals. He led the NBA in scoring once again with a 29.6 average, to go along with his usual accolades for the year overall. With five titles and several MVPs and Greatest of All-Time status, Jordan (it seemed) closed out the most prolific career in sports history like the legendary sports icon that he was in '97-98. Air Jordan's defining moment on the court was his best play ever. With time running out in Game 6 of the Finals in Salt Lake City, with the Bulls up 3 games to 2, Jordan stripped league MVP Karl Malone of the ball, dribbled down the court with the championship on the line, and drilled yet another game-winning shot to capture a championship.

Jordan retired and the Bulls were reorganized after the '97-98 season but he returned in 2001 at age 38 with the Washington Wizards. Jordan averaged 22.9 points his first year with Washington; and then 20 in '02-03 to end his career with a scoring average of 30.1 points in the regular season and 33.4 in the playoffs, both NBA records.

Jordan

MATT ZEIGLER

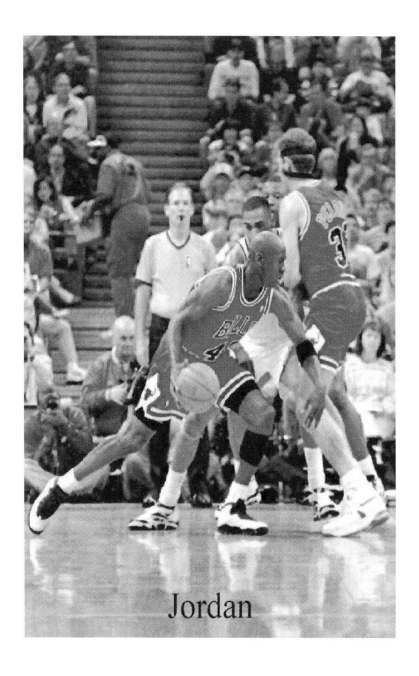

MATT ZEIGLER

Chapter 2 Sir Charles

Charles Barkley once called himself the NBA's 8th Wonder, considering the fact that he dominated a big man's position with a guard's height throughout his 16-year career. Barkley was an unstoppable force in the '90s with his aggressive, up-tempo style of play. Barkley played with a nasty attitude that he also lived by off the court, and he rarely apologized for questionable transgressions. Sir Charles put the power into power forward.

Although he was listed at 6'6", Barkley was actually 6-4, which comes up short for an NBA power forward. The player manning the "four spot" in the NBA could go anywhere from 6'8" to the 7-foot range typically. But Sir Charles was a dominant force even at 6'4", and a powerful 255 pounds of quick moves and fierce intensity. Barkley, from the very beginning back home in Leeds, Alabama, fought the odds, worked hard, took criticism and prevailed with a devastating game that featured rebounding prowess as well as dynamic scoring ability.

Barkley wasn't highly recruited during his high school years. In fact, he was the classic late bloomer that was signed by Auburn, a major Division I football power that withstood an underachieving basketball program. Underachieving until Charles arrived, that is. One of the knocks on Barkley early on was his weight, which, even he admitted, could get out of control at times and reached upwards of 280 pounds. But his weight issues did not prevent Barkley from performing at a high level. His dominating play as a collegian and pro proved that he certainly carried his weight well. He soon became the best player on Head Coach Sonny Smith's team, and he went on to lead the Southeastern Conference in rebounding three consecutive years. After three seasons of dominant SEC play, Barkley opted out of AU early after his junior season. Despite being cut from the final roster he had a stellar performance at the 1984 Olympic Trials. He then went on to be taken 5th overall in the NBA Draft by the Philadelphia 76ers.

From unknown, undersized, high school nobody to being a 1984 NBA First Round Draft pick was quite a climb, but Sir Charles took things in stride. But hitting life in the NBA's fast lane, on the defending NBA

Champions with legends such as Julius 'Dr. J' Erving and Moses Malone as teammates, was a quantum leap. However, Barkley knew he could play at the highest level of competition, just as he did in college.

Barkley's 16-year NBA career began in Philly (eight years) with four-year stopovers in Phoenix and Houston. After averaging 14 points and 10 rebounds a game at Auburn, in his prime Barkley was good for 25 points and 12 rebounds on average in the NBA. As a rookie he averaged 14 points and 8.6 rebounds per game, before improving to 20 and 12.8 his second season. By year three in '86-87 Barkley was a monster with averages of 23 points and 14.6 rebounds.

Meanwhile, the 76ers lost in the Conference Finals, semifinals and first round respectively his first three seasons. By the time the '87-88 season tipped-off both Dr. J and Moses were gone and Barkley was the unquestioned best player on the team. He responded with 28.3 points and 11.9 rebounds but the Sixers went 36-46 and out of the playoffs. Philadelphia rebounded in '88-89 with a 46-36 record as Barkley went for 25.8 and 12.5, but was defeated 3-0 in round one of the postseason by New York. For the '89-90 season Barkley led the 76ers to a 1st Place finish in the Atlantic Division with a 53-29 mark by again averaging 25 and 12. However, the 76ers lost out 4-1 to Michael Jordan's Bulls in the conference semifinals.

Barkley upped his scoring average to 27 points in '90-91 with 10 rebounds and 4 assists, but Philadelphia lost 4-1 again to the Bulls in the conference semifinals. Sir Charles led the Sixers in scoring and rebounding again the next season with averages of 23 and 11, but it was his last year in Philadelphia as the team fished 35-47. With the Phoenix Suns in '92-93 Barkley had another 25 and 12 season with 5 assists to earn the NBA's MVP award. Barkley's production slipped slightly during his next three years in Phoenix to 23 points and 11 rebounds, but the Suns remained contenders. However, they couldn't make it back to the NBA Finals, losing in the semis to Houston two years running. After a 41-41 finish in '95-96 and a first round playoff exit Barkley was off to Houston the next season.

With the Rockets Barkley was teamed with Hakeem Olajuwon and Clyde Drexler. The trio of stars led the Rockets to a 57-25 record in '96-97 and advanced to the Western Conference Finals, where they lost-out to Utah 4-2. Barkley was second on the team in scoring behind Olajuwon with 19 points per game during the regular season and led the team by averaging 13.5 rebounds. The Rockets went 41-41 and were out of the playoffs in the first round of '97-98 season. Scottie Pippen joined Olajuwon and Barkley in Houston for the strike-shortened '98-99 season and the Rockets finished 31-19; then suffered another first-round playoff exit. Barkley's last season in Houston in '99-00 was injury-plagued and he participated in only 20 games, but averaged 14.5 points and 10.5 rebounds.

Except for winning a championship Barkley accomplished it all during his superstar career. He was 1993 NBA MVP; had a career-high 56 points in a 1994 playoff game; was an 11-time All-Star; and is one of the league's top scorers all-time with more than 23,000 points. He was the leader and 'go-to' man on several contenders and was a dominant force in big-time basketball for almost 20 years, including his college days.

Barkley was also a member of the "Dream Team," the 1992 Olympic basketball squad that captured gold, plus Dream Team III which won gold in the 1996 Summer Olympics. He was also named one of the NBA's 50 All-Time Greatest Players in 1996. In 2006 Barkley was inducted into the Naismith Memorial Basketball Hall of Fame. When he retired there were only two men in NBA history with at least 23,000 points, 12,000 rebounds and 4,000 assists for their career, and Charles was one of them, along with the late, great Wilt Chamberlain.

Barkley

Chapter 3 The Admiral

At 7'1" tall David Robinson had a center's height but he also possessed the ability to run the floor and shoot from the perimeter like a forward. After being named a two-time All-American and Player of the Year as a senior he graduated from the Naval Academy in 1987, and went on to become the franchise for San Antonio. The Spurs drafted him No. 1 overall but due to his two-year naval service commitment, it wasn't until 1989 that he suited-up for San Antonio, a team that finished 21-61 the previous season.

The NBA of the 1990s featured plenty of smooth forwards gliding to the hoop or pulling-up for jumpers on the wing, as well as lightning-quick guards breaking down defenders with crossover dribbles. But the decade wasn't totally dominated by forwards and guards, a few Hall-of-Famers of the period were 7-foot centers. David Robinson, Hakeem Olajuwon and Patrick Ewing all hit the prime of their careers during the decade. The trio displayed different styles of play but all had the three required skills of a dominating big man: scoring in the low post; shot-blocking and rebounding.

Nicknamed "The Admiral" due to his naval background, Robinson came on station as a rookie in '89 and took command. Robinson's success would continue as he showed consistency all-around during his first seven years in the League. He averaged around 23 points and 12 rebounds during that span. Robinson led the Spurs to a 56-26 record and a Midwest Division title his rookie season, before falling in the semifinals of the playoffs. He was named Rookie of the Year as he averaged 24 points, 12 rebounds and almost 4 blocks per game and set many team records, in addition to being named an All-Star.

His second season was even better as he averaged 25 points and 13 boards and led the NBA with 4 blocks per game. He also was named First Team All-NBA and the All-Defensive First Team as well. During his fourth year in '92-93 he produced his normal 23 points and 12 rebounds per contest before exploding for a 29.8-point average to lead the NBA the following year.

The '94-95 season was his best yet, averaging 27 points, 10 rebounds and 3 blocks per game to earn MVP honors. He produced great numbers the next year also (25 points, 12 boards) and was named to his third Olympic Team, Dream Team III, which won Gold in Atlanta. He also won Gold with the original Dream Team in '92. The Admiral was cruising until a devastating foot injury put him out of action for the bulk of the '96-97 season. And without their leader the Spurs dropped out of contention.

The Spurs drafted 6'11" Tim Duncan first in the '97 Draft. And after years of coaching turbulence San Antonio replaced Bob Hill with Gregg Popovich after 18 games of the '96-97. 'Pops' brought stability to the organization for more than a decade; he also won multiple championships. Duncan teamed with Robinson to form the Spurs' version of the 'Twin Towers' and together they would lead San Antonio to its first championship. The addition of Duncan, a high-scoring, rebounding, shot blocking power forward/center in the class of Robinson himself, Robinson's numbers dropped to 21 points and 10 boards in '97-98, and to 15 points and 10 rebounds in '98-99. Duncan was a 21 and 12 All-Pro from the start with multiple MVPs and championships in his future. Some superstars have problems accepting a diminished role, but before Robinson became a superstar he had great character and an appreciation for teamwork.

Therefore, giving up his role as the main weapon on offense to a younger, up and coming star was no problem for Robinson. In fact, he welcomed Duncan aboard and showed him how to be a professional, which paid huge dividends for the entire organization. The '98-99 season was shortened to 50 regular season games due to a work stoppage for contract negotiations between players and management. But it didn't stop the Spurs and Robinson from claiming their first NBA title. Although he no longer was considered the Spurs' best player, he played a major factor in getting his team a championship.

If ever a player was deserving of a championship it was Robinson. Despite the NBA's image being scarred at times by unruly player behavior, Robinson always represented the NBA as a great citizen and good guy. He was blessed with natural height and ability, and he added a solid work ethic and strong character to become an all-time great. In addition to his incredible NBA career Robinson represented the US in three Olympic Games, winning two gold medals. Robinson's collegiate career is interesting being that as an athletic 7-footer with unlimited potential he could have taken an easier road to NBA success than the rigors of a military academy.

He was entrusted with the dreams and future of the Spurs and the city of San Antonio, and produced consistently until retiring in 2003. He started 64 games his final season and his 9 points and 8 rebounds on average per game were enough to help the Spurs their second another championship in '03. The Admiral retired with 20,790 points, 10, 497 rebounds and 2,954 blocks during his 14 seasons in the NBA.

David Robinson

Chapter 4 Pippen

In full stride and on the wing of the force that was known as Jordan, Scottie Pippen exploded from the shadows with his own Hall-of-Fame career. While His Airness became the NBA's greatest player ever Pippen carved out his own slice of glory. Jordan's prolific scoring and tight defense combined with Pippen's own all-around game to propel the Chicago Bulls to six championships during the '90s.

Unlike Jordan, an All-American at a basketball powerhouse, Pippen was an unlikely candidate to ascend to the top of the NBA kingdom. As a North Carolina freshman Jordan produced the game-winning shot for the 1982 NCAA Tournament Championship. Pippen, on the other hand, averaged 4 points a game as freshman at Central Arkansas, an NAIA school.

But by his senior season, the 6'7" forward had improved his average to 23 points with 10 rebounds. He became a first round draft pick in 1987, going to the Seattle Supersonics with the fifth pick, who later dealt Pippen to Chicago. The Bulls, despite those brilliant early years of MJ, wasn't yet a contender. Pippen didn't set the league on fire as a rookie either, averaging about 8 points and 4 rebounds as a reserve, but the Bulls finished 50-32, their first winning season since 1981. Pippen became a starter in the first round of the playoffs and responded well before the Bulls were eliminated in the semis by Detroit.

Pippen's game improved steadily from '88-90 and he became known for his all-around skills, averaging about 15 points, 6 rebounds and 5 assists. He could handle the ball like a guard, rebound, make steals and generally wreak havoc all over the floor defensively. He could stick a mid-to-long range shot on the perimeter or finish off a penetration move. Pippen and the Bulls as a whole improved steadily but the late '80s became a test of wills, a test of heart, the making of a dynasty forged in steel. The Bulls continued to win but in successive years they were literally "beaten down" by the Detroit Pistons in the Eastern Conference Finals. Worse yet, not only did the Bulls lose they, particularly Pippen, were labeled as soft for notwithstanding the physical style of the Pistons.

The dawning of a new decade became the awakening of an NBA giant. The 1990s would prove to be the era of Bulls supremacy. It also was the coming of age for Pippen. He began the decade with another solid all-around season in '90-91 and his production improved in the playoffs. He averaged 17.8 points during the regular season, but pumped in 21 per night in 17 postseason games, to go along with 9 rebounds, 6 assists and 2 steals. After finally overcoming the Pistons for the championship of the Eastern Conference, Chicago dispatched the Lakers 4-1 for the title.

Just as the Bulls fortunes soared the following season, so did Pippen's. He became a truly elite player; averages of 21 points, 7 rebounds, 7 assists and 2 blocks per game, All-Star game starter, All-Defensive First Team and All-NBA Second Team. At season's end, with another championship to savor, Pippen became a member of the original "Dream Team," which captured the gold medal at the 1992 Summer Olympics in Barcelona.

With Pippen and Jordan in their prime the Bulls were an unstoppable force that kept the winning and accolades flowing in '92-93. Despite the pressure associated with being the defending two-time champions Chicago withstood all challenges to claim its third world title. With three rings, a gold medal, All-Star and All-NBA recognition, Pippen's career was on a smooth course to the Hall-of-Fame. But the challenges of staying on top got even tougher, especially when Jordan retired at season's end.

Despite his accomplishments Pippen faced many hurdles in '93-94 with Jordan out of the lineup. Could he be the Bulls' "go-to" player? Could he be an effective team leader? Would the Bulls be a contender with Pippen as the leader? Could he lead the Bulls to another title? Although he had some forgettable moments, Pippen improved his production but the Bulls couldn't 'four-peat.' They were a contender though, winning 55 games in the regular season before falling to New York in the conference semifinals. As the Bulls' primary offensive weapon Pippen responded by averaging a career-high 22 points to go with 8.7 boards, 5.6 assists and 2.9 steals. He also was MVP of the 1994 All-Star game with 29 points, 11 rebounds and 4 steals.

Pippen wouldn't get another chance to see if he could lead the Bulls back to the top when Jordan returned near the end of the '94-95 season, setting the stage for the Bulls second championship run of the '90s. After Jordan came back and showed that he was still the man, Pippen proved to be better than he was during the first title run. He provided on average 20 points, 7 rebounds and 6 assists during the second three-peat as he continued to be a defensive stopper with scoring ability both inside and out. He seemed to be a confident, highly-productive secondary option.

With three more seasons of titles and individual awards, Pippen's NBA experience was reaching an iconic stature. His display of all-around talent earned him a place on the NBA's list of its 50 Greatest Players of All-Time in

1996. He also won his second gold medal as a member of Dream Team III that competed in the 1996 Summer Olympics in Atlanta. But after the Bulls' last title run in 1998, Pippen left Chicago and went on to play a year in Houston before signing with the Portland Trailblazers the following season, where he played until 2003. He played sparingly with the Bulls in '03-04 then retired.

Jordan left his imprint stamped in bold on the 1990s, but Pippen, a 2010 Naismith Hall of Fame inductee, represents much more than a footnote. He ended the decade ranked near the top of several statistical categories. He was tenth in points, 13,937, tenth in assists, 4,330, fourth in steals, 1,608, and third in minutes played during the '90s with 27,752. He ranked in the top 25 in games played and rebounds.

Pippen's also an all-time Bulls' great, ranking behind only Jordan in most categories. When all of the awards, rings, triple doubles, points, rebounds and all other stats are totaled, Scottie Pippen ranks as one of the best all-around players of the '90s and one of the greatest of all time.

Chapter 5 Thrill Hill

With a 6'8" frame built to slice, glide and penetrate, Grant Hill was a tough matchup for most defenders on the court in the '90s. Not only did he possess the ability to get to the basket and finish, he also could stick the jumper or dish off to a teammate. And his work ethic, unselfishness and personality made him a great team player and a fan favorite of the '90s generation.

Hill's collegiate career at Duke was productive beyond belief. Several NBA stars have captured NCAA titles, but not many have made it to the title game three times and claimed two wins. Yes, it was at Duke where the legend of Grant Hill was born. He arrived at Duke at the start of the decade in 1990. As a "Blue Chip" High School All-American he lived up to the hype by starting 31 games and helping lead the way to an NCAA Championship.

During his sophomore season Hill continued to improve and once again was a major cog in the wheel of the 1992 NCAA Tournament Champions. Hill's junior year didn't yield a three-peat championship, but his game was one of the best in the college ranks as he averaged 18 points, 6 rebounds and 3 assists; and displayed a great all-around command of the floor. As a senior Hill led the Blue Devils to the NCAA title game but lost to Arkansas, ending a brilliant collegiate career. Overall, after four years at Duke Hill had averages of 14.9 points and 6 rebounds, and finished his career sixth all-time in assist (461), and fourth all-time in both steals (218) and blocks (133), decisive proof of an all-around performer.

With the third pick in the 1994 NBA Draft Detroit selected Grant Hill to become a Piston. Despite a structured four years of disciplined basketball at Duke Hill spread his wings and "flew," in the more wide open, athletically inclined NBA game. With jumping ability on par with a young Jordan or Dominique Wilkins, "Thrill" Hill was a highlight showcase. With smooth, graceful yet powerful moves Hill would get to the basket and finish with either a soft touch off the glass, or deliver a dunk from a variety of angles; one or two-handed.

Hill, son of former NFL running back Calvin Hill, concluded his rookie year with a team-leading 19.9 points per game. He also led the team with 124 steals, and added 6 rebounds and 5 assist per game, proving he still produced more than just offensive fireworks. Hill was named Co-Rookie of the Year with Jason Kidd and led the NBA in All-Star Game votes, a first for a rookie. Despite Hill's spectacular debut, the Pistons finished the year out of the playoffs at 28-54.

Just as he improved on his freshman year at Duke Hill was even better his second season in the NBA. He became only the 15th player in League history to lead his team in points (1,618), rebounds (783) and assists (548), with per game averages of 20.2, 9.8 and 6.9 respectively. He also led the NBA with 10 triple doubles; was again named to the All-Star Team; and was a second-team All-NBA selection; plus a member of Dream Team II, which took gold at the 1996 Summer Olympics in Atlanta. Hill's outstanding play on the court translated into a 46-36 record and a trip to the playoffs for the Pistons, where they were swept 3-0 by Orlando.

After his early success Hill continued to improve his game. In 1996-97 he posted a career-high 21.4 ppg averaged (with 9 boards and 7 assists) as he once again led the Pistons in points, rebounds, assists, steals and minutes and had career high games of 38 points and 18 rebounds. He also was named First-Team All-NBA and started his third straight All-Star Game. The Pistons improved to a 54-28 regular season record, only to fall out of the postseason in the first round once again, 3-2 to Atlanta.

After three solid years of outstanding all-around play, Hill had evolved into the consummate professional by '97-98. His performance was consistent, with its usual flashes of awe. He once again led the team in most major categories with averages of 21 points, 7.7 rebounds, 6.8 assists and 1.77 steals. Hill also made his usual All-Star Game start and had 15 points, 5 assists and 3 rebounds for the East, along with second team All-NBA honors. But his team faltered for the most part, dropping out of contention to a 37-45 record and no postseason action.

Hill concluded the last two seasons of the '90s with his usual consistency and effective production, averaging 21 points, 7 boards and 6 assists in '98-99, while connecting for 25 ppg along with 6 rebounds and 5 assists in '99-'00. And he started in the All-Star Game both years, amongst his usual array of individual recognition. But Detroit's losing continued and Hill opted out of the Motor City following the season, signing with the Orlando Magic. The individual acclaim was great but records of 29-21 and 42-40 his final two seasons in Detroit deterred from an otherwise brilliant display of basketball ability.

Although his NBA career in the '90s didn't produce the team success on par with his NCAA career, Grant Hill was a star among stars with the game to back it up. He spent six years with the Magic but was severely limited in action, playing in only 135 games from 2000-2006 due to multiple ankle surgeries and complications thereof. His probability of making it all the way back to action was slim at best. He played in 65 games for Orlando in '06-07, averaging 14 points and 4 rebounds, then moved on to Phoenix. Against all odds he remained healthy in Phoenix through the 2010-11 season, averaging around 14 points and 5 rebounds for the Suns, and missed just three games from '08-11.

Grant Hill

Grant Hill

MATT ZEIGLER

Chapter 6 Dream Team

In April, 1989 basketball's worldwide governing body, the International Basketball Federation, changed its policy of prohibiting NBA players from competing in the Olympic Games. FIBA's decision opened the door for the creation of what is widely considered as the greatest basketball team ever: dubbed 'Dream Team.' The squad consisted of 11 of the NBA's best players, including several players that were considered the greatest of all-time at their position.

NBA All-Star games feature great players but the best talent is usually split evenly between two squads. Dream Team, however, was the best of the best. On paper DT was better than any of the NBA's previous champions, in any era. Better than any of the Bulls' championship teams in the '90s, better than Magic's best Laker team, or Bill Russell's most cherished Celtic relics. Not even Jerry West and Wilt Chamberlin's '71-72 Lakers could handle this team, theoretically.

Barcelona, Spain and the 1992 Olympics would be the stage. At guard the USA had the best 1 (point guard) and 2 (shooting guard) that ever lived in Magic Johnson and Michael Jordan. And Michael, of course, is greatly considered the greatest player at any position to play the game. Their 'backups' were perennial All-Stars John Stockton and Clyde Drexler. Stockton was to assists what Jordan was to scoring. He led the NBA in assists per game nine times and retired after 19 years with Utah as the all-time career assists leader with 15,806.

Larry "Legend" Bird headed up a diverse arsenal of forwards that could shoot with unlimited range on the perimeter or bang inside with power forwards and centers. The group included power forwards extraordinaire Charles Barkley and Karl Malone, along with small forwards Scottie Pippen and Chris Mullin, a perimeter shooter with deadly accuracy. If needed, Pippen or Mullin could also play shooting guard.

Patrick Ewing and David Robinson were all-world 7-foot centers that could score, rebound and block shots. Robinson could also run the floor like a forward. Duke's 6'11" forward Christian Laettner was the lone collegian to make the squad and he was the consensus NCAA Player of the Year for the reigning champions. Head Coach Chuck Daly's starting lineup was flexible, as was Dream Team's style of play. They could run and score in transition or slow it down and dominate with a half-court game, or simply fill it up from the outside. Dream Team could and did do it all. Even the competition knew it. They were just too big, too athletic, too fast, too experienced and too great.

Barkley was in prime form and provided a 24-point output in a 116-48 rout of Angola in the USA's first game. Croatia was supposed to provide the stiffest challenge, but were beaten down 103-70 the next day. Jordan took the leading scorer role in Dream Team's balanced attack with 21 points. Bird wasn't in top condition due to a back injury, but he connected for a team-high 19 points in a 111-68 crushing of Germany the third game. Brazil was under attack next and Barkley poured in a US Olympic record 30 points on 12-of-14 shooting to lead the charge in a 127-83 drubbing.

Wins over Spain, Puerto Rico and Lithuania followed with the same definite result of a 40-point blowout win. Croatia was back again for more in the gold medal game. If anything the Croats were consistent, they lost by 33 in the first meeting and 32 the second time around at 117-85. Jordan picked up his second gold medal in leading Dream Team with 22 points. Several records were shattered by Dream Team, including scoring (117 ppg) and a 43.8 point average margin of victory. American basketball was proven to be, beyond any doubt, as superior and a class above the rest of the globe.

After another roster of NBA players, Dream Team II, won gold at the 1994 World Championships, Dream Team III suited-up two years later in Atlanta for the Summer Olympics. The second Olympic team comprised of NBA players was minus Jordan, Magic, Bird, Drexler, Ewing, Mullin and Laettner from the original Dream Team. New additions included guards Anfernee Hardaway, Reggie Miller, Gary Payton and Mitch Richmond; Grant Hill at small forward; and centers Shaquille O'Neal and Hakeem Olajuwon.

Lenny Wilkens, an assistant on the '92 team, was head coach of the DT III. Wilkens was a true ambassador of the game who was legendary both as a coach and player. His long NBA career began in 1960 as a first round pick out of Providence of the then-St. Louis Hawks. In 15 seasons he averaged 16.5 points, 6.7 assists and 4.7 rebounds as a 6-1 floor leader. He was a player/coach in 1969 with Seattle when his coaching career began. Wilkens led the SuperSonics to the NBA Championship in 1979, and became the league's all-time winningest coach in 1995, and its first 1,000-game winner on March 1, 1996. Wilkens was selected as one the NBA's 50 Greatest Players of All-Time the same year. He was also named as one of the Top 10 NBA coaches of all-time, the only person to make both of the exclusive lists.

DT III was elite but not quite as dominant as the original version. International competition had also improved since the daily Barcelona bashings. Argentina fell by 28 points in the first game, but Team USA failed to score 100 points, winning 96-68. Angola followed suit with a 33-point loss, but Dream Team III managed 'only' 87 points. With concerns about the offense's production looming the century mark was eclipsed with a 104-82 win over Lithuania in the next outing. The 22-point loss was closest the competition came as they fell by an average margin of 31.75 points. China was massacred by 63, 133-70, with Pippen leading the way with 24 points.

After wins over Croatia, Brazil and Australia, DT II faced Yugoslavia for the gold medal. The Americans led by only 5 at the half and trailed 51-50 with 14 minutes to play. The NBA stars kicked into gear and went off on an 18-4 run, en route to winning 95-69. Robinson led the way with 28 points and 7 rebounds. Barkley once again led Dream Team in scoring average at 12.4, and rebounds with 6.6. He had averaged 18 points and 4.1 boards in '92. And although he played in only seven games he also led DT II in total rebounds with 46.

MATT ZEIGLER

Magic

MATT ZEIGLER

Chapter 7 The Dream

With an athletic 7-foot frame equipped with the quickness and agility of a forward, Hakeem Olajuwon mastered the center position in the 1990s. During a decade that featured several top centers, Olajuwon was considered by many to be the best in the league. Like most superstars of the decade Olajuwon's formative years in the NBA came in the 1980s. He also put together a spectacular college career before becoming the No.1 pick overall in '84, going to the Houston Rockets.

Dream, Olajuwon's nickname, is a native Nigerian who played soccer in his native country before discovering basketball and progressing onward to eventually become the most popular athlete in Houston. Olajuwon, a naturalized American citizen, lacked the experience of most collegians but developed into a force that helped lead the way to three consecutive Final Fours with the University of Houston. Although they would make it to the championship game twice the Cougars didn't claim a championship. But with a fast-paced kinetic style of play the Cougars, AKA Phi Slamma Jamma, were a national power and Olajuwon was considered the top NBA prospect on the planet, even selected ahead of Michael Jordan, who was taken third.

Back in 1984 the Rockets were grounded and needed a power booster. Stricken with hard luck in the playoffs, as well as eight losing seasons since the franchise moved from San Diego to Houston in 1971, Olajuwon was a symbol of hope. The savior was a local 7-foot foreigner with quick feet, great moves and shot-blocking ability. He was already a legend thanks to his college exploits. The city had adopted him as its hometown hero. And this was one American Dream that was fulfilled. He eventually delivered the goods with back-to-back titles in '94-95.

Olajuwon and the Rockets were an instant success story. During his rookie season he averaged 20 points, 12 boards and almost 3 blocks per game, while the Rockets went 48-34. Teamed with 7'4" Ralph Sampson, the "Twin Towers," Dream became an All-Star and was Second Team All-Defense and second to Jordan for Rookie of the Year. He increased his scoring (23 ppg) and shot blocking (3.4 per game) the following year, which would prove to be close to his career averages. But his best years on the court were clearly still to come. He developed high-twitch footwork and spin moves with the ball in the post, aka 'Dream Shakes,' that consistently separated Olajuwon from a defender to release a high-percentage shot.

As Olajuwon continued to gain honors and acclaim the Rockets continued to win, making it to the '86 Finals before falling to Boston in six games. He was named First-Team All-NBA as well as to the All-Defensive Team in 1987. Dream also proved to be a prolific at steals. He averaged 2.6 per game in '88-89, becoming the first player to record 200 steals and blocks in a season. Olajuwon averaged 24 points, a league-leading 14 rebounds and astounding 4.59 blocks (also topping the charts) per game during the '89-90 season. The Rockets went 52-30 in '90-91 as Dream averaged 21.2 points and 13.8 rebounds with 3.9 blocks, but were swept 3-0 by LA in the first round of the postseason.

With much past success Olajuwon and the Rockets slipped from contention in '91-92, finishing out of the playoff hunt for the first time in his career with a 42-40 record. He averaged 21 points, 12 boards and 4 blocks per game and made the All-Star Team, but his window for a championship was closing. With eight years of battles in the post behind him it appeared the Dream was slowing down, from a games-played standpoint. He missed 26 outings in '90-91 and 12 games the following season due to injury.

But The Dream would regroup for '92-93 and started all 82 regular season games. He averaged 26 points 13 boards and 4 blocks and was named First Team All-NBA and All-Defense to go along with the Defensive Player of the Year award. The Rockets captured the Midwest Division title with a 55-27 record, but fell to Seattle in the semi-finals of the playoffs.

In what would prove to be his best season all-around in '93-94 Dream earned the MVP award by averaging 27 points, 12 boards and 3.7 blocks per game. The Rockets finished the regular season with a franchise best 58-24 record. In the playoffs they defeated Portland in round one and then went on to defeat Phoenix and Utah to make it to the '94 NBA Finals, matched up against New York. It amounted to a battle or titans; Dream vs. the Knicks' Patrick Ewing, another 7-foot superstar center.

Ewing was an old nemesis. It was his Georgetown Hoyas that defeated Olajuwon's Cougars in the 1984 NCAA Finals. However, with the NBA's grand prize on the line it was Dream who captured the hardware, along with Finals MVP honors. The Rockets were finally NBA Champions after the seven-game duel, but defending the crown would be a tough challenge the upcoming year.

The Rockets ended the regular season at 47-35 and were seeded only sixth in the Western Conference for the postseason. They also were dealing with a lineup shuffle that brought in Dream's former Cougar teammate, Clyde

Drexler, and sent power forward Otis Thorpe to Portland. Houston opened with Utah and then fought off the Suns to make the Western Conference Finals. Against David Robinson and the San Antonio Spurs in the Conference Finals, Houston advanced once again to meet Orlando for the championship.

Orlando featured yet another dominant big man for Olajuwon to deal with in Shaquille O'Neal, and an All-Star caliber guard, Anfernee Hardaway, on the perimeter for Drexler. In a matchup of old pros vs. young guns the Rockets swept Orlando 4-0. Olajuwon picked up his second Finals' MVP Award in the process.

The Rockets couldn't "three-peat" but they continued to be in the hunt for a few years before closing out the decade in a rebuilding mode. Olajuwon continued to put up great numbers as he added more individual awards to go along with his two NBA crowns. Olajuwon was a 12-time All-Star and in 1996 he won a gold medal as a member of Dream Team III at the Summer Olympics in Atlanta. And he was also named in '96 as one of the NBA's 50 Greatest Players of All-Time. But by the end of the decade his production had dropped considerably as he dealt with injuries.

He was traded to Toronto in 2001 but finished his career as the Rockets' all-time leader in most categories, as well as being the NBA's all-time leading shot blocker with 3,830. He displayed great all-around talent with his scoring, rebounding, shot blocking and steals. And his two titles are proof positive of his ability to not only make himself the best, but also his team. He was enshrined into the Naismith Memorial Hall of Fame in 2008 after scoring 26,946 points and grabbing 13,748 rebounds.

Hakeem

Chapter 8 Magic

Earvin "Magic" Johnson only played one full season in the NBA during the 1990s but his legendary status as the best point guard in history made an impact in the '90s regardless. Magic was a main attraction of the NBA in the 1980s with the Los Angeles Lakers, particularly in their epic battles against Larry Bird's Boston Celtics. Magic was still going strong in the early '90s until a dramatic twist of fate prematurely ended his brilliant career.

At 6'9" he was and still is the tallest point guard in league history. With God-given height and talent Magic added desire and determination and a love of the game to capture multiple championships and MVP awards throughout his career. Johnson entered the national spotlight as a sophomore at Michigan State, where he captured the 1979 NCAA Tournament Championship over Bird and Indiana State. With the NCAA Championship and All-America status under his belt, Johnson left college two years early and became the first overall pick; selected by the Lakers in the '79 NBA Draft.

It took all of one season for Magic to prove that he would dominate the NBA. There wasn't a pass in basketball that Johnson couldn't execute; behind the back, off the dribble, alley-oop, and of course the no-look pass, which he executed with perfection. Magic could locate the open man and put the ball in his hands from anywhere on the court. And he was also deadly when leading a Lakers' fast break as he commanded the floor over much smaller guards.

With Magic in the backcourt and the legendary Kareem Abdul-Jabbar at center, the Lakers rolled to a 60-22 regular season record his rookie year, and all the way to the 1980 NBA Finals, where they matched up against the Philadelphia 76ers. Philadelphia had a strong team, led by Julius "Dr. J" Irving, but Johnson, once again, proved that he was more than a great player, he was 'Magic.' The Lakers were up 3-2 in the best-of-seven series, but Kareem was nursing a sore ankle and out of the lineup for Game 6 at the Philadelphia Spectrum. Enter Johnson, who took over at the center spot and completely dominated to the tune of 42 points, 15 rebounds, 7 assists and 3 steals, becoming the first rookie to win the Finals' MVP award.

With an NBA title to go along with his NCAA crown, combined with his All-NBA individual skills and honors, Johnson appeared to be well on his way to a highly successful and charmed career. But Johnson's quest, like that of athletes in all sports, would be filled with challenges, trials and tribulations. But through it all he always seemed to persevere and keep excelling. His second NBA season ended quickly with every player's worse nightmare: a serious injury. A bad knee sidelined Johnson 45 games during the regular season. In 37 games he averaged 21.6 points to go along with 9 assists and 9 rebounds, plus 3 steals, but the defending champs suffered an early exit from the playoffs.

In '81-82 Johnson and the Lakers returned to the Finals, where they defeated the 76ers 4-2 once again and Magic was named Finals MVP for the second time. But the championship season was also filled with controversy for Magic after it was alleged that he played a role in Head Coach Paul Westhead being replaced by assistant Pat Riley earlier in the season.

Philadelphia and Boston took down the Lakers to win titles in '83 and '84, but LA came back to capture NBA Championships in '85, '87 and '88. Magic averaged a career-high 24 points and 12 assists in '86-87, which led to his first regular season MVP award. He was also MVP in 1989 with 23 points and 13 assists to close out the 1980s.

With five NBA titles, two MVPs and numerous other awards Johnson, at 30 years old, entered the 90's with proven, championship-level skills. Magic won his third MVP award (22 points, 12 steals) for the 1989-90 season, but LA didn't make it back to the Finals after falling to Phoenix in the Western Conference Semifinals. For the ninth time in his career Johnson guided the Lakers back into the Finals the following year, but the Lakers were grounded by the "Air Jordan" express, as Chicago took the series and the title 4-1.

Johnson was well accustomed to making the news with his basketball exploits, but before the start of the '91-92 season, he announced to the world that he had tested positive for the HIV virus and was retiring after 12 glorious seasons. Although for the most part Magic's NBA playing career was finished, he continued to make headlines throughout the '90s. He was selected to play in the '92 All-Star Game and won the MVP award. It was his 12th All-star selection, despite not playing during the regular season. Magic also was part of the original "Dream Team," the gold-medal-winning 1992 US Olympic Basketball Team. Johnson assumed the role of head coach of the Lakers for the final 16 games of the '93-94 season but found life on the sidelines not to his liking.

After deciding not to be a coach any longer Johnson purchased a share of the team and became a part owner. Then Magic returned once again to the Lakers' lineup for the final 32 games of the '95-96 season, and the first round of the playoffs, where LA lost to Houston 3-1, before retiring a second and last time. Over the span of 13 seasons Johnson averaged 19.5 points and 7 rebounds. His average of 11.2 assists per game ranks first all-time in NBA history. His 10,141 assists rank 4th on the all-time list. He was enshrined into the Naismith Memorial Basketball Hall of Fame in 2002.

MATT ZEIGLER

Chapter 9 Worm

Rebounding is a gritty and unglamorous job that is pivotal to winning games but typically doesn't lead to superstardom. Until Dennis Rodman took rebounding and became the most unique superstar of the 1990s. He parlayed defense and command of the boards into overall team success; two titles with the Pistons during the 'Bad Boys' era, and three more with Chicago in the mid '90s. Rodman was an unlikely candidate for such lofty NBA success coming out of high school in the Dallas area in the early '80s. Rodman didn't even play high school basketball, standing just 5'11" as of graduation.

But a growth spurt that put 'Worm' in the 6'7" range led to junior college and a very productive NAIA career at Southeastern Oklahoma State. In three years Rodman averaged 15.7 rebounds and 25.7 points, surprising in that he never was much of an offensive threat in the NBA, but he proved that he could 'board with the best.' Rodman was taken in the second round of the '86 Draft and went on to a modest rookie year at small forward with averages of 7 points and 4 rebounds. The Pistons, under Chuck Daly's guidance, made it all the way to Eastern Conference Finals, falling to Boston in Game 7.

In year two of Rodman's career the Pistons were winning big but the best was yet to come. Dennis averaged a career-best 11.6 points with 8.7 rebounds while the Pistons finished the regular slate 63-19 before falling short in the NBA Finals to the Lakers. Rodman's improved production on the boards still didn't reflect his future dominance. He wasn't the biggest or stronger post player but what he had and continued to build upon was hustle, craftiness and doing whatever it took to defend or grab a rebound. His over-aggressive behavior drew technical fouls and ejections periodically, but 'Worm' made no apologies and continued to thrive as a Pistons Bad Boy.

With future Hall-of-Famers Isaiah Thomas and Joe Dumars, along with sharpshooter Vinnie Johnson, on the perimeter, combined with Rodman, Bill Laimbeer, Rick Mahorn and other assorted "bruisers" inside, Detroit crushed the opposition on its way to two consecutive titles to close out the '80s and begin the '90s with championships. Rodman averaged 9 points and 9 rebounds from '88-89, and was named to the All-Defensive Team. Although he had limited offensive skills he led the league with a 59.5 percent field goal percentage.

He then followed that year up with averages of 8.8 points and 9.7 rebounds and was named the NBA's Defensive Player of the Year, along with All-Star Game selection. Detroit was the reigning back-to-back NBA Champions in '90-91 and Rodman's game would continue to get even better. However, the Pistons were not destined for more championship glory in the decade. With Air Jordan in full flight the Bulls dominated the NBA on their way to their first three-peat, followed by a second trifecta.

Detroit compiled a 50-32 record in '90-91 before falling to the Bulls in the Eastern Conference Finals. Rodman's rebounding average jumped to 12.5 per game in '90-91, then Rodman's rebounding became second to none. With an average of 18.7 rebounds per game in '91-92 Rodman led the NBA in rebounds per game for the first of seven consecutive seasons, spanning three teams and three rings. Standing 6'7", not exactly towering by NBA standards, Rodman ruled the glass with an uncanny knack for knowing where the ball would be and beating everybody else to it. He had 39 games in which he grabbed 20 or more rebounds.

He followed up his 18.7 average with 18.3 rebounds per game during the '92-93 season, but the Pistons slipped to 40-42. Rodman was traded to San Antonio before the start of the '93-94 season. His two-year stint in West Texas featured both success and failure. It also yielded the beginnings of what became a sideshow. Rodman was known on the court as an energizer who didn't mind getting the dirty work done. He continued that trend in San Antonio by averaging 17 rebounds a game in two seasons with the Spurs.

And as he began to wear his hair in bizarre colors and added more and more tattoos and body piercings to his anatomy Rodman's behavior became more erratic on and off the court. Rodman was more than just a little eccentric, but the fans absolutely loved him and 'Worm' became one of the NBA's most popular players. He also continued to be the game's top rebounder.

Rodman's antics created a stir for sure but he didn't let showmanship get in the way of serious board work, most of the time. He averaged 17.3 boards per game in '93-94 and 16.8 the following year. After Houston claimed top status in the state, division, conference and NBA two years running Rodman found himself back in the Eastern Conference the following season, and this time around with his old rivals, the Chicago Bulls. Before the Bulls became champions in the '90s they had to go through the Detroit Pistons. The battles were outright brutal, with Rodman delivering several hard fouls to the Bulls' Michael Jordan and Scottie Pippen. Chicago eventually prevailed after years of beat-downs, but many skeptics wondered if the Bulls could embrace the former villain.

Not only did the Bulls and Rodman work out their differences they dominated the league together. It didn't take long either. In '95-96 the Bulls won a record 72 regular season games and the NBA Championship. The show continued to roll along the following season with Rodman's 16 boards a game once again topping the NBA as the Bulls repeated.

With three-peat on the mind of Bulls' faithful Chicago rolled all the way to the finals again in '97-98 and they didn't disappoint by claiming yet another title. Rodman had another spectacular year by averaging 15 boards a game. Although he didn't appear to be showing much decline in his game '97-98 proved to be Rodman's last full season of production. He logged 23 games with the LA Lakers in '98-99 and 12 with the Dallas Mavericks the following year to finish out his career on a down note. Regardless, he averaged 14 rebounds in the dozen games with Dallas at age 39. For his career he totaled 11,954 boards.

His behavior both on and off the court made many enemies for Rodman. But when all the votes were counted Rodman was rightfully inducted into the Naismith Memorial Hall-of-Fame in 2011. He wasn't much of a scorer over his 12 full seasons in the NBA, but in his prime Rodman's rebounding and defense were on an All-NBA level, and he showed consistent year-in, year-out dominance, as evidenced by his seven consecutive rebounding titles. But the most valid reason for Dennis' greatness is the fact he was a major contributor on five NBA Championship teams. Wild behavior, multi-colored hair, body piercings and tattoos can't overshadow the legacy of a champion.

Rodman/Hakeem

Chapter 10 Mr. Big Shot

An NBA player's value is measured in numbers; averages of 20 or more points in conjunction with 10 or more rebounds or 8 assists is worthy of All-Star recognition, and form the foundation for a championship. And 25-30 points a game propels a shooter to the All-NBA level. Robert Horry never came close to averaging those kinds of numbers over the course of an 82-game season. The most points he ever averaged were 12 in '95-96, and his 7.5 rebounds per game in '97-98 were a career-high.

Throughout the decade he averaged around 8 points and 5 rebounds with a few assists, steals and blocks per contest. But Horry was one of those players who couldn't fully be judged by a box score. Horry was a quality NBA player that displayed a lot of versatility in his game. This versatility enabled Horry to start or come off the bench and make major contributions; at small or power forward.

However, Horry finished his career at the top amongst his counterparts in the one stat that counts most; championships won. The 6'10" forward was a major part of back-to-back championships at Houston before winning back-to-back-to-back titles with Los Angeles from '00-02, and two more with San Antonio in '05 and '07. Horry's seven rings rank higher than some of the greatest players ever, including Jordan, Magic and Bird. And he wasn't just along for the ride, he was a starter in Houston and the sixth man for LA and the Spurs.

At 6'-10" Horry had the size and ability to score, rebound and block shots inside, but he could also step out to the perimeter and bury a three-pointer. He also was a skilled ball handler and passer for a man his size and played with a hard-nosed attitude. Horry learned old-school discipline from his Andalusia High School coach, Richard Robertson, and at Alabama under Wimp Sanderson. In college he averaged 15.8 points and 8.5 rebounds per game as a senior and was an All-SEC selection.

With great size, scoring ability and defensive skills, Horry possessed prime NBA talent that was acquired by the Houston Rockets with the 11th pick in the 1992 NBA Draft. He quickly stepped into the starting small forward's spot and produced effectively as a rookie, averaging 10 points, 5 rebounds, 2.4 assists and 1 block per game. The Rockets enjoyed a successful year also, winning 55 games and the Midwest crown before advancing to the semifinals in the playoffs.

With a solid rookie season behind him in which he started all 79 games that he played in and made the All-Rookie Second Team, it appeared Horry's career was on the right track. He produced similar numbers and the retention of his starter's spot the next season. Surprisingly, he was traded to the Detroit Pistons for Sean Elliot midway through the '93-94 season. It was a mild shock considering that both the team and the player were progressing along well. Elliot was a scorer and possessed a more diverse offensive game than Horry, which was the main factor in the trade. The trade proved to be a hasty move, but business was business and Horry found himself in Detroit. But the trade was later nullified when Elliot failed his physical. Once he returned back to Houston Horry made the most of his bizarre circumstances and stepped right back into his starting role. The Rockets repeated as Midwest champs and then dispatched Portland, Phoenix and Utah to meet New York for the title in the Finals.

It was a classic battle for the title as New York's Patrick Ewing matched up against the Rockets' Hakeem Olajuwon. The two big men battled inside with Olajuwon getting the edge. After a seven-game grudge match Houston remained standing for the title. Taking another championship appeared to be out of reach for the Rockets the following season. They finished only 47-35 and were seeded sixth in the West. They also had a few kinks to work out due to a late season trade that sent mainstay Otis Thorpe away and brought in Clyde Drexler. But thanks in no small part to Horry's strong postseason performance, the Rockets pulled off the repeat by defeating Orlando 4-0 in the Finals.

Horry averaged 17 points per game in the series and hit a number of clutch shots throughout playoffs. Horry played one more season in Houston and averaged career highs in points (12 ppg), rebounds (5.8), assists (4), steals (1.63) and blocks (1.54) but it wasn't enough to keep him a Rocket. He moved on Phoenix for 32 games of the '96-97 season, before being traded to LA. Horry was switched to power forward as a Laker, where he averaged a career-best 7.5 rebounds per game in '97-98.

But battling in the paint reduced his offensive effectiveness by diminishing three-point opportunities. He attempted only 93 treys that season, the lowest since his rookie year, and hit only 19 for a 20 percent success rate. His last year in Houston he hit 142-of-388 attempts (36 percent). After seeing his numbers dip to career-low levels and being assigned to a backup role in '98-99 it appeared Horry's best days were behind him. But as a sixth man for the Lakers from '99-'02 Horry found himself in another title run.

With Shaquille O'Neal inside and Kobe Bryant all over the Lakers had all of the offensive firepower they needed. What Horry provided was playoff savvy and doing a lot of the little things that paid off big. It came in the form of a three-pointer here, a steal, rebound or block there. His ability to connect on a game-winning shot in the playoffs earned him the nickname 'Big Shot Rob.' After moving on to the Spurs he continued to play a pivotal role off the bench, including clutch shots in the playoffs, leading to titles six and seven in '05 and '07. He retired after the '07-08 season after 16 years of play.

Horry didn't start but at the end of the game when it all was on the line he was usually on the floor; a good defender on one end, a good decision maker with the ball on the other and a formidable presence everywhere in between. He never made an All-Star Team, or an Olympic team and he probably won't get any consideration for the Naismith Hall-of-Fame. But there are not too many players who have better, more rewarding careers than Horry when you add-up his seven championship rings.

Horry

Chapter 11 Ewing

Patrick Ewing entered the national spotlight as a young, energetic shot-blocking force·in the early '80s, before blossoming into a NBA superstar of the '90s. And along the way he persevered through good times and bad to become the New York Knicks' most revered player. Ewing was a dominating center that could rebound, block shots and score with an arsenal of post moves and jump shots. He was Coach John Thompson's most productive player during his four-year stay at Georgetown. Over that span he averaged 15 points and 9 boards while leading Georgetown to three NCAA title games; capturing a championship in 1984. He also finished his college career as the Hoyas' all-time leading shot blocker and rebounder and second all-time scorer.

After graduating in 1985 the two-time All-American became the property of the New York Knicks, who selected him first overall in the NBA's first draft lottery. He became an instant success; averaging 20 points, 9 rebounds and 2 blocks to earn Rookie of the Year honors. He also made the All-Star Team, starting a run of 10 straight selections. Ewing would continue to average around 20 points, 8 boards and 3 blocks per game during his first four years in the league, but team success faltered. The Knicks finished 23-59, 24-58 and 38-44 respectively during his initial three years in the NBA, before breaking out to a 52-30 record in '88-89. A primary reason for the losing seasons was the fact that despite Ewing's stability at center, the Knicks as a whole were anything but stable. Ewing would play for eight different coaches during his Knicks career, including six his first seven seasons in the NBA, along with constant personnel changes on the court.

Ewing's diligence paid off in '89-90, his fifth year. He developed a deadly baseline jumper in the NBA that helped push his average to 28.6 ppg. His rebounding jumped from 9 to 11 per game, and he averaged nearly 4 blocks per game. His scoring and blocked shots were Knicks' single season records and led New York all the way to the conference semifinals, where they fell to Detroit. Ewing earned his first All-NBA First Team selection for what would be his finest season as a professional.

Although he would never reach averaging 28 ppg again, Ewing nevertheless gave outstanding performances year-in and year-out for the balance of the decade. From the 1990-91 season all the way to decade's end in '98-99, Ewing averaged around 23 points, 11 boards and 2.5 blocks per game, with similar playoff averages. And to go along with his All-Star production the Knicks became perennial contenders in the Eastern Conference.

But despite Ewing's 26 points and 11 rebounds New York slipped to 39-43 and a first-round playoff loss in '90-91. But hope for the future came in the form of former Lakers' coach Pat Riley for the '91-92 season. Ewing, grown fully accustomed to his superstar role, averaged 24 points, 11 boards and 3 blocks and the Knicks turned it around with a 51-31 record. But in the playoffs they ran into the Chicago Bulls in the conference semifinals. It was a long, brutal series that went the seven-game distance, but Ewing and the Knicks once again came up short.

Ewing was good for 24 and 12 in '92-93 and the Knicks compiled a 60-22 record and seemed poised for a title run. They appeared up to the challenge after defeating Indiana and Charlotte in rounds one and two, before taking command of the Bulls 2-0. But the inspiration of Michael Jordan propelled the Bulls to victory in the next four games to win the East and the eventual championship.

The Knicks were right back in contention during the '93-94 campaign. Jordan was retired and the Bulls' reign would be temporarily halted. With a power vacuum to fill the Knicks stepped up and went 57-25 during the regular season and was primed for the postseason. In the playoffs they stopped New Jersey in the opening series and faced the hated Bulls next. It was a typical Eastern Conference playoff war; the teams slugged it out for seven games. When the smoke cleared the Knicks were on top. But with Indiana up next the Knicks couldn't celebrate long. The Pacers also proved to be worthy adversaries, pushing the Knicks to seven games also before falling.

The Houston Rockets were champs in the West, which provided a classic "Big Man" matchup for the title; New York's Ewing vs. Houston's Hakeem Olajuwon. It was another grueling series but this time around the Knicks lost-out in Game 7, thanks primarily to horrendous perimeter shooting. The two superstar big men battled it out in the paint with the edge going to The Dream. Olajuwon scored more points while Ewing grabbed more rebounds and rejected more shots. Ewing was a star throughout the playoffs nonetheless, averaging 22 points and 11 rebounds in 25 games. He also set records for most blocks in a Finals game (8) and a Finals series (30).

The Knicks rebounded with 55 wins the following year, but the NBA Finals became an unattainable goal, particularly after Riley resigned at season's end. With a new coach, former assistant Jeff Van Gundy, and ever-changing lineup Ewing's championship dreams appeared to be fading, but his game was not. He still was one of the top players in the NBA and was named in 1996 as one of the 50 Greatest Players in NBA History. That honor, in addition to his NCAA accomplishments and two Olympic Gold Medals, won in 1984 and in again in 1992 with the original "Dream Team," secured Ewing's legacy.

But like all great players he yearned for an NBA title and another shot came at a most unlikely time. It was the shortened '98-99 season and the Knicks barley made the playoffs; qualifying as the 8th seed with a 27-23 record. Remarkably they would make it all the way to the NBA Finals but Ewing was out of action. Due to an Achilles tendon injury he left Game 2 of the East Finals against Indiana and was out of action for the remainder of the playoffs, which the Knick loss to San Antonio in the NBA Finals 4-1.

Ewing left New York to play for Seattle in 2000, and finished his career with Orlando in 2002. In 17 seasons he scored 24,815 points, secured 11,607 rebounds and rejected 2,894 shots. Ewing was enshrined into the Naismith Memorial Hall of Fame in 2008.

MATT ZEIGLER

MATT ZEIGLER

Chapter 12 All-Stars

The NBA's East vs. West battle for supremacy is waged in June during the Finals; but a preliminary skirmish takes place in February at the annual All-Star Game. Although defense is a luxury for All Stars offense goes off the charts. Its exhibition status does not warrant aggressive defensive play but offensive fireworks are guaranteed. All-Star Games are made for showcasing one-on-one offensive skills. Quick shots and ball-hogging are standard modes of play. Win or lose at least 120 points of fast-paced hoops is a must for each team. And an All-Star Game MVP trophy or two is owned by most legendary ballers.

Magic Johnson's game-high 22 points won MVP honors in the 1990 game as the East prevailed 130-113. In addition to superstar matchups on the court, such as Patrick Ewing and Hakeem Olajuwon in the post, two high profile coaches were also in the spotlight. LA's Pat Riley and Detroit's Chuck Daly were adversaries in the two previous NBA Finals. Los Angeles took the series 4-3 in 1988, followed by the Pistons' 4-0 sweep the following year.

Riley and Daly were championship-caliber coaches with contrasting personalities and methods. Riley represented West Coast flash; his four-time champion Laker teams of the '80s were known for a flashy, high-energy fast-breaking style of play, better known as 'Showtime.' Daly's Pistons won back-to-titles in '89-90 with a rugged style of play that matched their coach and blue-collar city.

1990 EAST All-STARS: (Starters listed first) Michael Jordan, Charles Barkley, Larry Bird, Isiah Thomas, Patrick Ewing, Joe Dumars, Reggie Miller, Dennis Rodman, Dominique Wilkins, Kevin McHale, Robert Parrish, Scottie Pippen.

1990 WEST All-STARS: James Worthy, Magic Johnson, A.C. Green, John Stockton, Hakeem Olajuwon, Clyde Drexler, Tom Chambers, Rolondo Blackman, Karl Malone, Lafayette Lever, David Robinson, Chris Mullin, Kevin Johnson.

Sir Charles was a great scorer and rebounder and he proved it in the '91 game on his way to being named MVP. Barkley grabbed 22 boards to go along with 17 points to lead the East to a 116-114 win. Jordan brought his usual 'A-Game' to the court and gave his home state fans in Charlotte, North Carolina a show. He was the game-high scorer with 26 points.

Boston's Larry Bird was selected as a starter for the East, but missed the game because of a chronic back injury. The three-time NBA champion and MVP and would retire in 1992 due to his back problems. In 13 legendary seasons with the Celtics he averaged 24 points, 10 rebounds and 6 assists and became a Hall-of Famer in 1998.

1991 EAST All-STARS: Michael Jordan, Charles Barkley, Patrick Ewing, Joe Dumars, Bernard King, Larry Bird, Dominique Wilkins, Alvin Robertson, Kevin McHale, Brad Daugherty, Hersey Hawkins, Ricky Pierce, Robert Parrish.

1991 West All-STARS: Magic Johnson, David Robinson, Chris Mullin, Karl Malone, Kevin Johnson, Clyde Drexler, Terry Porter, John Stockton, Tom Chambers, James Worthy, Kevin Duckworth, Tim Hardaway.

The age of Jordan's rule was in full force by 1992, but it was over-shadowed in the All-Star Game by Magic Johnson's MVP performance. His 25 points and 9 assists were instrumental as the West crushed the East 153-113.

Magic had retired before the start of the season due to his infection with the aids virus but was voted into the game as a starter. Utah's Karl Malone, who was also selected to start for the West, was critical of Johnson's decision to play. Malone questioned if other players were at risk themselves while playing with/against Johnson. He played in the game but was criticized for what many believed to be an overreaction.

1992 EAST All-STARS: Michael Jordan, Charles Barkley, Patrick Ewing, Isiah Thomas, Scottie Pippen, Joe Dumars, Dennis Rodman, Michael Adams, Kevin Willis, Reggie Lewis, Brad Daugherty, Mark Price, Larry Bird, Dominique Wilkins.

1992 WEST All-STARS: Magic Johnson, Karl Malone, Chris Mullin, Clyde Drexler, Chris Mullin, Tim Hardaway, John Stockton, Otis Thorpe, James Worthy, Jeff Hornacek, Dikembe Mutombo, Dan Majerle.

The West won the '93 All-Star Game with a close 135-132 victory. Malone and Utah teammate John Stockton earned Co-MVP honors. Utah's Delta Center, Malone and Stockton's home court, hosted the event. Malone had 28 points and 10 boards, Stockton added 9 points and 15 assists.

Both players would end the decade as two of the game's all-time greats. Malone, a two-time league MVP, was a 6-9, 260-pound force of a power forward. During the 1990s he accumulated more points (21, 267) and minutes played (29,982) than any other player, and finished second in rebounds with 8,393. Stockton led the NBA in assists per game nine times and averaged 12 assists with 15 points in '93.

Jordan led the East in scoring with 30 points. Shaquille O'Neal was a big rookie out of LSU and started at center for the East and registered 14 points in his first of 12 All-Star games.

1993 EAST All-STARS: Michael Jordan, Scottie Pippen, Shaquille O'Neal, Isiah Thomas, Larry Johnson, Patrick Ewing, Detlef Schrempf, Brad Daugherty, Joe Dumars, Mark Price, Dominique Wilkins, Larry Nance.

1993 WEST ALL-STARS: Karl Malone, Charles Barkley, Clyde Drexler, John Stockton, David Robinson, Tim Hardaway, Hakeem Olajuwon, Terry Porter, Sean Elliot, Shawn Kemp, Danny Manning, Dan Majerle, Chris Mullin, Mitch Richmond.

Scottie Pippen was a three-time NBA Champion in 1994 and after leading the East to a 127-118 win he became an All-Star Game MVP as well. He scored 29 points and added 11 rebounds.

Pippen was in the spotlight since Michael's retirement after the Bulls clinched their third straight title in '93. He didn't lead the Bulls back to the Finals but he was the star of stars on All-Star Sunday 1994. New York's Patrick Ewing and Cleveland's Mark Price each came off the East bench with big 20-point contributions for the eastern stars.

1994 EAST ALL-STARS: B.J. Armstrong, Scottie Pippen, Derrick Coleman, Shaquille O'Neal, Kenny Anderson, Charles Oakley, Horace Grant, Mark Price, Patrick Ewing, Mookie Blaylock, John Starks, Dominique Wilkins, Alonzo Mourning.

1994 WEST All-STARS: Shawn Kemp, Hakeem Olajuwon, Karl Malone, Clyde Drexler, Mitch Richmond, Danny Manning, Kevin Johnson, John Stockton, Latrell Sprewell, Cliff Robinson, David Robinson, Gary Payton, Charles Barkley.

The West was back on top in 1995 after they clubbed the East 139-112. Mitch Richmond didn't start the game but came off the bench and got red hot. He poured in 23 points by hitting on 10-of-13 shots for MVP honors. Richmond was a 6'-5" scorer at shooting guard who posted a scoring average of 21 points or higher in each of his first 10 seasons. He averaged 22 points and was Rookie of the Year in 1988-89 at Golden State. Together with Chris Mullin ·and Tim Hardaway he was part of 'Run TMC,' the Warriors' high-scoring trio of the early '90s.

1995 EAST ALL-STARS: Anfernee Hardaway, Reggie Miller, Grant Hill, Scottie Pippen, Shaquille O'Neal, Larry Johnson, Vin Baker, Patrick Ewing, Joe Dumars, Dana Barros, Tyrone Hill, Alonzo Mourning.

1995 WEST All-STARS: Dan Majerle, Latrell Sprewell, Charles Barkley, Hakeem Olajuwon, Shawn Kemp, John Stockton, Mitch Richmond, Dikembe Mutombo, Gary Payton, Karl Malone, Detlef Schrempf, David Robinson, Cedric Ceballos.

After a two-year absence Jordan was back in 1996, leading the East to 129-118 victory. Jordan's 20 points were enough to win the MVP award, though many thought that Shaq's 25 was more deserving of the honor. O'Neal was in the last of four brilliant years with the Orlando Magic.

The 7'1 300-pound center averaged 27 points, 12 rebounds and 2.7 blocks a game with the Magic before signing a free-agent contract with the Lakers in '96. When he landed on the West Coast Shaq continued to dominate and by the end of the decade he was a regular season, All-Star Game and Finals MVP. And the Lakers became champions once again behind the 'Shaq Attack.'

1996 EAST ALL-STARS: Michael Jordan, Scottie Pippen, Penny Hardaway, Shaquille O'Neal, Grant Hill, Terrell Brandon, Patrick Ewing, Alonzo Mourning, Reggie Miller, Glenn Rice, Juwan Howard, Glen Rice.

1996 WEST ALL-STARS: Charles Barkley, Clyde Drexler, Shawn Kemp, Jason Kidd, Hakeem Olajuwon, Karl Malone, Sean Elliott, Gary Payton, John Stockton, Mitch Richmond, Dikembe Mutombo and David Robinson.

MVP Glen Rice held the hot hand in the 1997 game, scoring an All-Star record 20 points in the third quarter alone, helping drop the West 132-120. Jordan had 14 points and 11 rebounds and 11 assists for the first triple-double in All-Star Game history. Rice was a 6'8" jump shooter that could score readily from outside. 'G Money' left Michigan in 1989 as the Big Ten's all-time scoring leader, and with an NCAA Championship for good measure. Rice had developed into a 20 ppg scorer by his third year with Miami and maintained the pace for the next six years. After a six-year stint in Miami he played three years with the Hornets. He was with the Lakers in 1998 and although his scoring dipped to 16 points a game in 1999-00 he earned an NBA championship.

The NBA's 50 Greatest Players of All-Time were featured at half time of the '97 All-Star Game. The team wasn't announced in 1996 without controversy. One omission, Dominique Wilkins, was particularly unwarranted. The 'Human Highlight Film' averaged 25 points and 7 rebounds a game over his 15-year career.

O'Neal, who made the team after less than five years in the league, perhaps drew the most animosity regarding his place on the team. Of course after he later became an MVP and four-time champion his selection appears to have been a correct choice.

1997 EAST ALL-STARS: Michael Jordan, Scottie Pippen, Grant Hill, Penny Hardaway, Joe Dumars, Tim Hardaway, Terrell Brandon, Dikembe Mutombo, Glen Rice, Vin Baker, Christian Laettner, Chris Webber, Patrick Ewing, Charles Barkley.

1997 WEST ALL-STARS: Shawn Kemp, John Stockton, Gary Payton, Hakeem Olajuwon, Latrell Sprewell, Mitch Richmond, Eddie Jones, Kevin Garnett, Karl Malone, Detlef Schrempf, Tom Gugliotta, Shaquille O'Neal, Charles Barkley, Clyde Drexler.

NBA's 50 GREATEST PLAYERS of All-TIME: Kareem Abdul-Jabbar, Nate "Tiny" Archibald, Paul Arizin, Charles Barkley, Rick Barry, Elgin Baylor, Dave Bing, Larry Bird, Wilt Chamberlain, Bob Cousy, Dave Cowens, Billy Cunningham, Dave DeBusschere, Clyde Drexler, Julius Erving, Patrick Ewing, Walt Frazier, George Gervin, Hal Greer, John Havilcek, Elvin Hayes, Magic Johnson, Sam Jones, Michael Jordan, Jerry Lucas, Karl Malone, Moses Malone, Pete Maravich, Kevin McHale, George Mikan, Earl Monroe, Hakeem Olajuwon, Shaquille O'Neal, Robert Parrish, Bob Pettit, Scottie Pippen, Willis Reed, Oscar Robertson, David Robinson, Bill Russell, Dolph Schayes, Bill Sharman, John Stockton, Isiah Thomas, Nate Thurmons, Wes Unseld, Bill Walton, Jerry West, Lenny Wilkens, James Worthy.

Jordan picked up his third All-Star MVP trophy in 1998 as the East took it 135-114. He scored 23 points with 6 rebounds and 8 assists. Kobe Bryant, winner of the '97 Slam Dunk Contest, started his first All-Star Game. Bird returned as the coach of the East team after leading Indiana to the Eastern Conference's best record at the All-Star break.

Karl Malone was in the West' starting lineup alongside the 19-year-old Bryant. Kobe eventually became a multiple champion and MVP; and the NBA's most exciting player as well. Malone was a solid old pro who was in his 13th season. The Mailman called for the ball in the low post at one point during the contest, but was waved-off by Kobe, who wanted it cleared out for a drive to the hoop.

Players not getting the ball or even being 'frozen out' is not unusual in the All-Star Game, but it's normally the veterans that keep the ball from the young guns. Kobe's perceived arrogance was the start of a changing of the guard in the West. Malone and the Jazz represented the Western Conference in the Finals, where they fell to the Bulls. Behind Kobe and Shaq the Lakers would eventually become best in the West.

1998 EAST All-STARS: Michael Jordan, Grant Hill, Penny Hardaway, Shawn Kemp, Dikembe Mutombo, Tim Hardaway, Steve Smith, Rik Smits, Antoine Walker, Reggie Miller, Jayson Williams, Glen Rice.

1998 WEST All-STARS: Shaquille O'Neal, Kevin Garnett, Kobe Bryant, Gary Payton, Karl Malone, Vin Baker, Tim Duncan, Nick Van Excel, Jason Kidd, Mitch Richmond, David Robinson, Eddie Jones.

The 1998-99 NBA season began with a lockout, resulting in a 50-game regular season and no All-Star Game. Stars such as Allen Iverson, Allan Houston, Michael Finley and Vince Carter would have to wait until Y2K to make their all-star debuts. Eastern Conference squads won six of the nine All-Star Games of the 1990s. They also won seven of the decade's Finals' matchups.

Steve Smith (8)

Van Exel

Van Exel

Kevin Johnson

MATT ZEIGLER

Allen Houston

MATT ZEIGLER

Kevin Johnson

Van Exel

About The Author

Matt Zeigler worked eight years as a photojournalist and sportswriter in the newspaper industry before embarking on an author's path. In addition to extensive coverage of youth and high school sports he traveled extensively throughout the Southeast covering the greatest athletes of American sports.

Zeigler has also published *Three Block War: U.S. Marines in Iraq* and *Sports Shooter: A Photographer's Story*. *Sports Shooter* was a 1st Place winner in the 2010 USA Book News Best Books Awards. Zeigler currently lives in central Alabama with his wife Glenda and son Matt.

Bibliography

Atlanta Hawks
Atlanta-Journal Constitution
Baseball-Reference.com
Basketball-Refernce.com
Chicago Bulls
Detroit Pistons
Houston Chronicle
Houston Rockets
Los Angeles Lakers
Naismith Memorial Basketball Hall of Fame
National Basketball Association
New York Knicks
The Birmingham News
The New York Times
Phoenix Suns
San Antonio Spurs
Seattle SuperSonics
The Washington Post
USA Basketball

Printed in Great Britain
by Amazon